A German Bomber
on Worthing Soil

"A German Bomber on Worthing Soil"
is an original idea by the author Graham Lelliott.
It contains a detailed study of the German Heinkel
111P bomber, which was shot down at High Salvington,
Worthing, West Sussex on Friday 16th August 1940.

Graham Lelliott

A German Bomber on Worthing Soil

10 Digit ISBN 0-9553893-0-5
13 Digit ISBN 978-0-9553893-0-6

Published by;
Graham Lelliott, 3 Busticle Lane, Sompting,
Lancing, West Sussex, BN15 0DH, England
Website: www.grahamlelliott.co.uk

First edition printed in 2006.
Second edition printed in 2007.
This is a third edition also printed in 2007.

Printed and bound by;
CPI Antony Rowe, 48-50 Birch Close,
Eastbourne, East Sussex, BN23 6PE, England
Tel: + 44 (0)1323 434700
Website: www.antonyrowe.co.uk

This book is dedicated to my grandmother, Johanna (Mary) Kennard, who passed away in February 2005. She would have been very proud to see the completed project in print.

Contents

Introduction

On Friday 16th August 1940 my grandfather witnessed the German Heinkel 111P bomber get shot down at High Salvington and was able to obtain armoured cabling and two pieces of metal from the plane as souvenirs.

My grandfather first told my brother and I about this plane crash many years ago when we were small children. When we visited our grandparents we would often look at the aircraft pieces, as for some reason it always excited us that our grandad had witnessed a German plane get shot down. To my brother and I World War Two sounded so exciting and at that age it never occurred to us how horrific it really was.

While visiting my grandparents in March 2004, having forgotten about the story for many years, the Heinkel incident suddenly came up in conversation. On returning home I began thinking on how it would be a great idea to research this incident fully and try to find out as much as I possibly could.

Because it was the first enemy aircraft shot down over Worthing and the wreckage was easily accessible to the public, it has become one of the most exciting highlights of the Battle of Britain for many Worthing residents. As a result I have been able to put together a detailed study of the incident, which includes eyewitness accounts, official reports and photographs past and present. I had even tried my utmost to get in contact with the three airmen that survived the crash. Sadly this was not possible.

All photographs, documents, eyewitness accounts and other sources used have been acknowledged and copyright permission granted. However if something has been overlooked then this is down to human error and is completely unintentional.

It has taken two years to research this Heinkel crash, as spare time is a bit of a rarity. It has at times become quite a challenge, mainly due to conflicting stories and the lack of detail in documenting such incidents. Nevertheless, I have had great pleasure in researching this incident and feel that this project is now complete.

Graham Lelliott

The Battle of Britain

The High Salvington Heinkel bomber was shot down during the height of the Battle of Britain and because of this I feel that it is necessary to give a brief account of the conflict between Britain and Germany. This brief account also includes the build up to the Battle of Britain.

Before the Battle of Britain started, Hitler's armies had already stormed across Europe and by June 1940 had conquered Belgium and the Netherlands. They were closing in on France at a frightening speed. Back in England, British Prime Minister Winston Churchill was committed to help his allies and as a result, loyally sent planes from the Royal Air Force over the English Channel and into war torn Europe.

Royal Air Force Chief Marshall Sir Hugh C. T. Dowding was very concerned. He was losing men and planes in France at an alarming rate and he feared the Royal Air Force's ability to protect England itself was being compromised. On the 6th May 1940, he communicated with British Prime Minister Winston Churchill and asked that the number of aircraft sent to France be limited. Dowding's concern was initially met with resistance, but wiser counsels soon prevailed and Great Britain ceased sending planes to Europe.

Towards the end of June 1940, Hitler's forces rolled through Paris and his victory over France was complete. It was at this stage that Hitler fixed his eyes on England. Prime Minister Winston Churchill was well aware of Hitler's intentions and prepared England for a conflict later known as "The Battle of Britain".

The Royal Air Force Fighter Command considered itself adequate to defend Great Britain from a German invasion, even though the German air force, the Luftwaffe had more aircraft. British fighter planes, such as the Spitfire and the Hurricane would be responsible for destroying the Luftwaffe's Messerschmitts, Stukas, Heinkels, Dorniers, Junkers and Focke-Wulfs which at the time amounted to a total of 2,800 aircraft.

Although the Luftwaffe may have had more aircraft, the Royal Air Force could rely upon some secret technology. This included a sophisticated early warning radar system, which enabled the Royal Air Force to concentrate large numbers of fighters at specific and vital areas to engage the Luftwaffe.

On 10th July 1940 Hitler sent the first aircraft over the channel to England. Over 100 aircraft were reported and were noted to be paying particular attention to East coast shipping, Portland and Portsmouth. During the two month long campaign, the Royal Air Force would be involved in exceptionally fierce dogfights and England's countryside would soon be littered with many shot down German planes, both bombers and fighters.

On the 31st October, the Battle of Britain fizzled out. Germany had exhausted every tactical alternative after being deprived of their best chance of victory, by the inept decision from their Supreme Command to attack the city of London rather than continue with the direct offensive against Fighter Command and its ground installations.

Hitler strongly believed that his forces would easily defeat the Royal Air Force Fighter Command and by most accounts they should have done this. Hitler grossly underestimated the resolve and competence of Dowding and his Royal Air Force.

Thanks to the confidence and belief in their cause of the RAF pilots, and Dowding's resolve leadership, the Royal Air Force managed to defeat the Luftwaffe, handing Germany its first major setback in the war. Dowding was given much credit for the success of his role, although he deflected this credit to those he felt better deserved it.

The Incident in Detail

Friday 16th August 1940 was a fairly sunny summer's day with a touch of haze in the sky. The plotting tables had remained quiet until about 11:00am although an hour later this would drastically change and at this stage of the Battle of Britain the airfields were still the main target.

That afternoon Heinkel 111P bomber, registration G1+FR, works number 1582 of the 7. /Kampfgeschwader 55 bomber unit left its base in Villacoublay, France. Onboard was 20 year old Leutnant Rudolf Theopold (pilot), 25 year old Unteroffizier Rudolf Hornbostel (observer), 22 year old Gefreiter Helmut Glaser (wireless operator), 30 year old Unteroffizier Albert Weber (flight engineer) and 23 year old Gefreiter Johannes Moorfeld (gunner). Their service numbers in the above order were; 58246/199, 58246/403, 58246/128, 58246/123 and 58246/411.

The above photograph shows a Heinkel 111P bomber similar
to the High Salvington plane. (Mr S. Hall)

Its bombs were successfully dropped on its target, the Great West Aerodrome, now known as Heathrow Airport. On returning the Heinkel was intercepted at 4:55pm over Brighton, East Sussex at 2,500 ft by three, Royal Air Force Supermarine Spitfires MK1's. These British fighters, which were being flown by 602 Squadron, City of Glasgow, Blue Section, were based at RAF Westhampnett near Chichester.

With the RAF planes behind pumping them full of machine gun fire, the bulk of the heavy medium sized German bomber would most certainly be no match for the fast and responsive British Spitfire.

Another photograph of a Heinkel 111P bomber, this time of one in flight. Once again this is not the High Salvington plane. (Mr S. Hall)

I would presume that the enemy knew that they would not last in the air for long before having to bail out or crash land. This thought can be the only explanation for the Heinkel not heading out over the English Channel to return to its airfield in occupied France. Landing in the sea was something the German airmen obviously wanted to avoid.

Instead the Heinkel turned and flew in a westerly direction along the coast for approximately ten miles to Worthing, probably trying to out manoeuvre the Spitfires, and trying to avoid the machine gun fire. It is also quite possible to assume that by this time, the gunner of the Heinkel, Johannes Moorfeld, was also firing back at the Spitfires from his glazed turret at the top of the bomber.

Once it reached Worthing, eyewitness reports show that from here the Heinkel turned north. Bill Baldwin, a Worthing resident remembers the Heinkel and the RAF fighters fly over his house in Mardale road. He had to run to a north-facing window in order not to miss all the action.

From here however, eyewitnesses recall seeing only one Spitfire in hot pursuit of the German bomber. I presume that by now it was evident that the Heinkel was struggling to stay in the air and that it would soon be on British soil. With this in mind, it would seem as though two of the 602 Squadron Spitfires decided to withdraw, leaving the "kill" to 25 year old Flight Lieutenant Robert Findlay Boyd, service number 90165, in Spitfire N3227.

The German bomber and the lone Spitfire then flew over my grandfather and his friend who were at Offington Lane and flew on northwards towards the Oval in Findon where resident Brian Chappell saw the two planes from his home.

At this point the Heinkel turned southwest, flew over Rogers Farm and crash-landed at High Salvington in the field between Honeysuckle Lane and Cote Street. It had landed completely intact with its wheels still retracted and faced southwest in the direction of Highdown Hill.

The Spitfire's pilot would most likely have then circled the crippled plane before flying off and returning to RAF Westhampnett. Once Robert Findlay Boyd had landed he completed the Combat Report which stated; "Sighted E/A (Enemy Aircraft) approx 1,000 ft above and coming towards us. Blue 1 did climbing turn and delivered beam attack, followed by Blue 2 who stopped one motor. Successive attacks were delivered by section until E/A crashed in waste ground approx 4 miles north of Worthing. Landed at 17:45 hours".

Seconds before the bomber landed it was noted that Royal Artillery personnel, who were manning a twin Lewis machine gun on the west side of Cote Street had seen the Heinkel come into view and span the gun round in order to get a shot at the enemy. A few rounds were spent before the plane crash-landed.

Although the plane had landed completely intact, Johannes Moorfeld and Albert Weber had died. The Volksbund Deutsche Kriegsgraberfursorge records state that Johannes Moorfeld died on the way to Worthing Hospital, although all other records state he died in the crash landing. Two other airmen were badly injured but the fifth airman escaped with only minor cuts and bruises.

The High Salvington Heinkel 111P bomber can be seen above. Particular attention is being made to the inside of the aircraft, making me wonder if the German airmen were still in the plane when this photograph was taken. (Worthing Herald and Gazette / Portsmouth Publishing and Printing Ltd)

On Wednesday 21st and Friday 23rd August 1940 both the Worthing Gazette and the Worthing Herald reported a shot down Heinkel. During World War Two, newspapers were forbidden by censorship regulations to identify specifically the sites of where a British or German plane had come down.

It was even forbidden to identify places that had been bombed during an air raid. Although photographs of planes and bombed buildings could be published, captions would read, for example "The end of a Heinkel, which crash landed in a Sussex field" or "A house damaged during a recent Nazi air raid on a south coast town".

It would have been very unlikely for a Worthing paper to show a picture of a bombed house or downed plane in Brighton and so Worthing residents would often recognise the photographs of incidents that had occurred in their hometown. As a result of this censorship regulation the only thing that links these reports with the High Salvington Heinkel are a few photographs of the plane and the names of some of the crew.

The Worthing Gazette also talks about another German bomber which was shot down in the area, a Junkers 88, and so some of the reports may be connected with this. However I wish to add the newspaper reports to this project because it is possible that they are related to the High Salvington Heinkel.

The Worthing Gazette reported; People on the ground who watched the dogfight said that the Heinkel came so low they could see the gunner. A machine gun bullet passed through an upstairs bedroom window of a house and through the wall into a room behind. Fortunately the occupants were taking cover downstairs. Over sixty tiles had to be replaced on the roof the next morning. Many people in the village, thinking the air raid was over, came outside at the moment the Heinkel was overhead.

The Worthing Herald reported; Children picked up spent machine gun bullets and fragments of fuselage from the roadway. One resident found that a bullet had landed on his bed. Four people in a car which was being driven along the main road near the scene of the battle stated that the plane was forced so low over the road that the driver had to stop the car and the occupants had to dive for cover in a hedge.

The Worthing Herald continued to say; A woman and a 10-year-old girl were picking black berries near the spot the German bomber was brought down. She explained that; "We crouched under bushes in a disused chalk pit. The planes seemed to circle round and round the lip of the pit and we expected every minute to see the bomber crash near us. We could see the men in the machines, so low they were.

When things had quietened down a bit we discovered we were lying in a bed of stinging nettles, but in the excitement we hadn't noticed that discomfort. The little girl behaved marvellously, although it was a terrifying experience. When we climbed out of the pit a man asked us if we had seen a plane crash. At that moment we saw the wing of the machine not a hundred yards away. We were told that one of the crew was badly wounded, so I took the little girl away".

Another photograph of the High Salvington Heinkel can be seen below. By the time this photograph was taken, the German airmen had already been taken away. Looking at the photograph it does appear as though the Heinkel's registration is G1+FH. Official reports state the registration is G1+FR. I can only presume that the bullet hole at the top of the letter has flaked the paint off, making it appear as though it is a letter H and not the letter R. Note all the bullet holes in the rear, which according to the RAF report, amounted to 303. (Worthing Herald and Gazette / Portsmouth Publishing and Printing Ltd)

The Worthing Gazette also said; Two local women, each with two children who were out in the country at the time the Heinkel came down, had an alarming experience. When they saw it being chased they took the only cover available, some bushes.

One of them said afterwards; "Bullets whistled through the bushes all around us as the planes came over. We were too busy keeping the children undercover to notice which planes were which. My little boy thought it was great fun. This Heinkel circled round at low altitude with the Spitfire pouring machine gun bullets into its tail and eventually crashed, finishing with its nose in some bushes five yards from a chicken coop".

A local man told a Worthing Gazette reporter; "I was working when the German plane came over. It was very low and one of our fighters was flying just above it. I ran to get my glasses and said to my mate – if you've never seen the swastika before there is one now. Some soldiers in a field fired at it with their rifles and a machine gunner in the plane fired back at them. The Germans circled round a wood and then came down".

Once again it is not clear whether these reports are concerning the High Salvington Heinkel, although one may have noticed that these eyewitnesses explain that the German bomber circled before crash landing. I can only presume that the crew knew that they were going down and wanted to choose an appropriate field in which to crash land.

The perspex nose which offered the crew superb visibility can be seen above. Part of one of the engines can be seen at the bottom left of the photograph. (Worthing Herald and Gazette / Portsmouth Publishing and Printing Ltd)

Bob Richards of Beechwood Avenue, Worthing, explained to me; "That Friday afternoon I was in a corn field at the Gallops, High Salvington at a place known locally as the Seven Sisters. I was shooting rabbits with Mr Holmes, the police superintendent of Worthing. I must add he was off duty at the time. A team of farm workers were also in the field and were collecting all the corn. As a result, the rabbits were being disturbed and this made shooting the rabbits much more exciting.

Suddenly this large German bomber came speeding towards us, having just come from the Rogers Farm area. A British fighter was close behind and at the time I believed it to be a Hurricane. We all ran to take cover under the tractor and trailer, which was parked in the field. As the planes flew over we watched as the two planes disappeared over High Salvington. It was evident that the enemy had gone down so Mr Holmes and I decided to put our best foot forward and walk to the top of the hill to locate the plane".

Although none of the crew bailed out, a silk parachute can be seen in the foreground of this photograph. This was one of the first "souvenirs" to be taken, which is no surprise as silk was a sought after commodity in WW2. The British Censorship Bureau has obliterated some of the plane's registration on the photograph itself for security reasons. This was due to the Control of Photography Order 1939.
(Worthing Herald and Gazette / Portsmouth Publishing and Printing Ltd)

Miss J. Naish of Pavilion Road, Worthing remembers; "My mother and I were returning home in the early evening, walking south along Honeysuckle Lane, High Salvington. Suddenly, an enormous plane with machine guns blazing flew across the lane, knocking the top off a young oak tree in a shower of leaves and twigs. We hurried to a clearing in the gorse bushes and there, on the ground, was this huge plane, a Heinkel bomber. It seemed odd to see the swastika on the fuselage in the English countryside. We saw the Heinkel again some days later and someone had cut the swastika out of the tail as a souvenir".

At the same time, Worthing resident Derek Round was also taking a walk along Honeysuckle Lane when the Heinkel flew over and landed very heavily in the field. He rushed to the plane to help two badly wounded members of the crew out, but a few minutes later British soldiers, who were manning an observation post further up the hill, appeared and took the German crew and Derek Round prisoner. They presumed he was one of the crew and although he was in civilian clothes, he was in the plane and talking to them in German.

Mr Richards and Mr Holmes continued across the open fields to the top of High Salvington and about ten minutes later arrived at the scene. Mr Richards noticed that one of the airmen had a Luger pistol in his hand and when approached, was reluctant to hand it in.

Soon after, the Home Guard, policemen and many others had arrived on the scene including a woman doctor who was called to attend the incident. Derek Round was unable to convince the soldiers that he was a local man, so they locked him in the ambulance with the five German airmen and took them to Worthing Hospital. Derek Round was then taken to the police station where he was interrogated and finally driven home.

Throughout the ordeal he was very impressed with the calmness of one of the German airmen, whom he presumed to be the pilot, Rudolf Theopold. The pilot first asked where they were, then could he give them a cigarette and finally, would he retrieve his cap which he had left in the cockpit, as he thought it unlikely he would be able to obtain a replacement for a while. He also bitterly complained that it was very un-British for the fighter plane to have continued pumping bullets, just as his plane was crashing.

A few days later Derek Round was allowed to visit the two badly wounded airmen, now in Worthing Hospital, and took them some cigarettes and sweets, much to the disgust of the other patients in the ward.

Shortly after the airmen had been taken away and although soldiers and the police were at the scene, it appears that they did nothing to stop souvenir hunters pulling the plane to pieces. Mr Richards tried to get the radio transmitter from the plane as a souvenir but was spotted by a policeman and was kindly asked to return it to the cockpit.

Children gather to obtain a piece of the German bomber.
(Worthing Herald and Gazette / Portsmouth Publishing and Printing Ltd)

John Goodwin of Goring-by-Sea remembers cycling up to see the bomber. He explained; "Along with other boys, I had with me various tools. As we approached the plane, the noise of everyone banging away and trying to detach bits as souvenirs I was not to hear again until I ended up some years later as a signals sergeant in a tinsmiths shop in Baghdad".

The A.F.S collect donations with an appeal for a Spitfire fund.
(Worthing Herald and Gazette / Portsmouth Publishing and Printing Ltd)

Allen Woods, who now lives in Rustington, was 17 at the time. He visited the crash site shortly after the plane had come down and remembers walking the length of the "crash trail" up towards Honeysuckle Lane.

He explained that; "After striking the ground the bomber had cut a 400-yard trail, going towards the chalk pit at the top of Cote Street, gradually gouging deeper tracks in the turf and scrub before it came to rest. I can confirm that the crew did not bail out, as I saw two of them near the aircraft. I was struck with the tallness of one of the Germans and was very surprised that they were wearing brown overalls and not the blue and grey ones I somehow expected to see".

Two soldiers examine the silk parachute. Note the crowd in the background.
(Worthing Herald and Gazette / Portsmouth Publishing and Printing Ltd)

Brian Cracknell was in Wigmore Road, Broadwater when he witnessed the Heinkel fly over. The three RAF Spitfires were on its tail, although as explained earlier, two of these British fighters would later withdraw.

Brian explains; "I was a 9 year old schoolboy on summer holiday at 6 Wigmore Road, Broadwater. The day was brilliantly sunny and although sporadic warnings sounded from time to time no one sheltered, unless there was really close ack-ack or bombs.

I was in the front garden when I heard the sound of aircraft and machine gun fire coming up rapidly from the south. Forgetting all precautions I stood on our small garden wall to see if I could see anything. Suddenly a Heinkel 111 swept across the roof tops at about 500 feet, very closely followed by three Spitfires, some 50 yards between the nearest.

The aircraft flew directly along the line of Wigmore Road and bursts of machine gun fire could easily be heard above the engine noise. The thing I recall most was the brilliant colours of the aircraft. For although camouflaged, the roundels, crosses and squadron markings of the machines were incredibly bright in the sunshine.

Later that day I walked with friends to where it had gone down. The plane was guarded by three soldiers. One of them pulled out some clothing from the nose, it was a pair of long johns come siren suit, pale cream in colour. There was a bullet hole in the lower stomach region and a huge area of blood staining around this. Everybody cheered like mad when he held this up. This was repeated several times when other groups of civilians visited the wreck".

Ernie Parsons, who at the time was living in Sompting, remembers that his wife's two uncles, who were in the same regiment in the regular army, stood guard over the Heinkel. Mr Parsons attended the North Lancing Evacuees School and was fortunate to visit the Heinkel with his teacher, Mr Fido (this may have been his nickname), and other members of his class.

Having taken money in for the bus fare they took the bus to the top of Salvington Hill and on arrival the teacher cut a propeller blade off using a hacksaw, which he had taken with him. Mr Parsons and other members of the class also took home a souvenir to remember the German bomber. Incidentally the teacher's propeller blade was taken home and displayed above his mantle piece.

John Sylvester, who now lives in Billingshurst, West Sussex, explained to me that he was 13 years of age at the time and living in the house opposite Cissbury Garage in Findon Valley. He recalls; "I was at home that particular Friday with some friends of mine and on hearing growling engines, ran out to the road (A24).

A Heinkel was flying north following the A24 Worthing to Horsham road and had a Spitfire behind but slightly above it. The Spitfire was pumping bullets into its tail and as a result we had to dive for cover behind the garden wall. The planes flew past and instead of watching where the planes were going, we began picking up the empty shells.

I later heard that the Heinkel had crash-landed at the top of High Salvington and so I decided to go and find the plane. Once there I used my army knife to get a souvenir piece of aluminium fuselage. My next door neighbour, who was in the Auxiliary Fire Service, also visited the site. He came back with blood stained harnesses, which he took from inside the cockpit. Sadly I no longer have my Heinkel souvenir".

From this photograph, one can clearly see the overall shape and size of the plane. It is also worth noting the amount of prickly gorse and turf in the foreground, which may have helped the plane slow down before coming to rest in the hedge. (Mr C. Ellis)

Peter Trounce, who now lives in Toronto Canada, kindly sent me an E-mail which explained; "I, with my family (I was 17 at the time) were living on Hayling Rise, High Salvington and I was on school holidays then. There had been an air raid warning, but that was so usual we didn't take much notice. Then we heard planes and quite a lot of low height machine gunning. I recall being surprised that the firing sounded like only one or two guns, not a RAF fighter's 8 guns, so maybe that was the Heinkel.

When it stopped we went outside. I expected to see the house covered with bullet holes! I don't recall how I knew where it had crashed but I walked to beyond the convenience store west of the windmill and saw a plane down facing southwest with its wheels still retracted. The plane was not in any way demolished. There was a local policeman there keeping people away because it was thought it may still have bombs on board.

There was a dead body, which had been taken and put in the back of a truck nearby. I didn't see the rest of the crew. I recall the front of the glasshouse canopy forward of the pilot's position was splattered with blood. Being wartime, people were actively discouraged from being nosy about things, so I assume that the RAF came and somehow took it all away later.

I remember the Heinkel was one of the German oddities in World War Two because they had never developed heavy bombers like the British Lancaster bomber, they only used these much smaller two engine planes. A lot of their ideas were weird, like the too clever V2 rockets.

I also seem to recall that soon after the Heinkel incident there were a load of bombs that were dropped on the east side of Hayling Rise, north of Woodland Avenue, in what was then an open field".

Mr G. Wheeler of Penfold Road, Worthing remembers that he was in Findon Valley at the top of Vale Drive on the Downs with some others that hot day and recalls that several other planes were also shot down that very same day. To see any aerial activity must have been quite exciting, for Mr Wheeler was, like most schoolboys, into aircraft recognition.

Mr Wheeler explains; "I still have the remnants of a book from all those years ago. It was simply called "Aircraft Recognition" and was mostly silhouettes. I also used to enjoy drawing planes, which I thought were quite good, but mine were not plastered round the school walls like others were".

Evelyn Smith of Worthing also visited the crash site and explains; "I was 14 at the time and had just left school. I lived with my mother and father at Durrington and being on the hill, we had a grandstand view of the dogfights and enemy planes coming in over the sea. We were often reprimanded by the air raid wardens for racing up and down the garden path shouting encouragement to the Spitfires overhead.

On the day the Heinkel came down, my mother and I set out to walk to Cote Street and after a lot of wandering around we came upon it, quite huge and awesome, laying belly down in the grass. Around it was a looped roped fence on short posts about eight inches off the ground and one rather forlorn looking Home Guard. When we enquired, he told us the crew had been taken to hospital with two dead.

On the ground were masses of broken windows that had shattered on impact. I bent down and picked up a piece about two inches in size and was informed it would cost me sixpence for the Spitfire fund, which I duly put into a tin placed near a post. I was a little disappointed at not being able to see inside the plane as one small boy gleefully said to me that he climbed in before the Home Guard had arrived and there was a lot of blood and gore".

The front of the plane. Note the opened hatch on the left. (Mr C. Ellis)

A closer view of the tail section. Note the Heinkel's works number 1582.
(Worthing Herald and Gazette / Portsmouth Publishing and Printing Ltd)

Alan Townsend from East Preston, Littlehampton cycled up to see the German bomber with a friend of his. When they arrived the Home Guard were already at the scene. Mr Townsend remembers seeing two airmen sitting on one of the wings drinking what looked like cups of tea.

Lionel Burns, of Goring Road, Steyning, remembers that this dead rabbit was found under the wreckage shortly after the plane crash-landed. (Worthing Herald and Gazette / Portsmouth Publishing and Printing Ltd)

Barbara Chipper from Goring-by-Sea went up to see the plane too. She explains; "I remember it well, as I was one of the many school children who rushed with great excitement to view it and if possible, obtain a souvenir. I remember taking home my booty, a small strip of metal from a wing, I think, and placing it on the mantelpiece. It gave off a peculiar pungent smell and, to my disgust, my mother made me remove it to the garden shed".

A policeman stands alone. (Amberley Working Museum)

Two policemen and a bystander appear to be showing some interest in the gun turret. (Amberley Working Museum)

A RAF Intelligence Officer also visited the site to evaluate the plane, just in case there was anything new onboard that they needed to know about. The oil, fuel, machine guns, ammunition and other items of interest were retrieved from the plane, although it is not clear whether this happened before or after the crowd pulled the plane to pieces.

A group photograph. (Amberley Working Museum)

The RAF Intelligence Report concerning this visit and showing an incorrect registration number (should be G1+FR not G1+SR) stated the following; "He.111. Crashed on 16.8.40. at Salvington Hill, Nr. Worthing. Markings G1+SR (S in white; spinners white). Engines D.B.601. Shot down by fighter action; between 300 to 400. 303 bullet holes in rear. No armour was perforated. Six machine guns salved and approximately 50 magazines. Aircraft badly damaged but not disintegrated. Crew of 5 killed or wounded".

One can see that the policemen are once again in the spotlight.
(Amberley Working Museum)

Worthing resident, Freddie Feest visited the Heinkel on the Saturday. He explained; "I remember riding my bicycle across Worthing and to the top of Salvington Hill to see the first German bomber to be shot down over Worthing. But this was the day after the Heinkel had crashed and I felt lucky to still get a small souvenir of the German bomber because most of what was removable had by this time disappeared".

Roger Moulds recalls; "We all went off to High Salvington where the German Heinkel bomber had crashed, and I remember being lifted up so that I could see into the cockpit. I don't know what I had expected to see, but there was nothing glamorous about it, and I felt sorry for the people who had been in it".

Ronald Ham also visited the site and remembers; "We often watched dog fights between the RAF fighters and the Luftwaffe bombers over the town during the Battle of Britain. Along with many others, dad and I went to see the Heinkel 111 that was shot down and crashed at the top of Honeysuckle lane in August 1940. It attracted a large crowd, many of whom took a bit of perspex or metal work as a souvenir".

Valerie Kay, once a Worthing resident but now living in Hayle, Cornwall, contacted me to tell me what she had experienced. She explained; "I was 12 and living in Broadwater at the time. My brother was 15. We both rode our bicycles up to the crash site. I don't remember how we knew where the plane had come down, I think we just followed the crowd.

We did pass many people with bits and pieces from the plane, most noticeably bits of green painted metal. They all seemed to be very excited. We were able to climb on the plane and have a good look over it, but for some reason we did not return with any souvenirs.

I remember that my brother would often watch the dog fights over Worthing and would jump up and down with excitement when the enemy went down. My mother would always get angry with him and would explain that it was someone's son".

My grandfather recalls an ex colleague of his also visited the downed plane. He found a pair of black airman's boots in the cockpit and took them home for his father, who fortunately had the same size feet. When he returned to school he exaggerated his story by telling his classmates that he had found a severed foot in one boot.

The Heinkel remained on site for a few days and was then collected by the Brighton based haulage contractor, A.V.Nicholls and Co. Flatbed trucks were used to remove what was left of the plane, although before this the bomber was cut into manageable sizes for transportation.

Whilst the aircraft was being cut up, it caught fire, presumably as vapour in the fuel tanks ignited. Black smoke filled the sky and the fire brigade were called. Instead of the fire engine approaching the field from Honeysuckle Lane, they made the mistake of driving up Cote Street and as a result were unable to get anywhere near the plane. During this time a human chain was made to Cote Bottom Farm and buckets of water were passed along the chain back to the plane. This proved to be unsuccessful and so the Heinkel was left to burn. When the fire brigade finally arrived at the scene the fire had burnt itself out.

The haulage contractors can be seen above at the crash site.
Members of the Home Guard can also be seen. (Mr C. Ellis)

Like all downed British and German aircraft in Southern England, the Heinkel was taken to No.49 RAF Maintenance Unit at Faygate near Horsham, West Sussex. The mangled wrecks were collected here in the fields literally next to the Southern Railways goods yard at Faygate station. The High Salvington Heinkel would have been dismantled and then sent out with other wreckage by rail to be melted down and used again by the aircraft industry.

These unidentifiable piles of mangled aircraft wreckage are the intermingled carcasses of British and German warplanes lost in battles across Sussex and collected together at No.49 RAF Maintenance Unit at Faygate. (Mr A. Saunders / Middleton Press)

The photograph below shows how the site of No.49 RAF Maintenance Unit has now been taken over by small industrial units. (Authors Collection)

The three surviving crew members, Rudolf Theopold, Rudolf Hornbostel and Helmut Glaser were later sent to a Prisoner of War camp in Canada, although before this they were probably sent to Camp 11 at Trent Park in London for interrogation. It is unclear when they were sent to Canada, however in the Worthing Gazette dated Wednesday 4th September 1940 it explains that a 22 year old German airman whose plane crashed a couple of weeks back was still in Worthing Hospital being treated as an honourable enemy.

It is not known who this chap was but the information given does suggest that it could have been Wireless Operator Helmut Glaser. The Worthing Gazette explained; A Hospital official told a reporter that anonymous letters had been received from people who had not taken the trouble to check up on the rumour in the town that the German was being pampered.

"Some of the letters were disgusting. There was no truth at all in the rumour. We did not treat him as a German, or as an airman, or as a Protestant, or anything else. To us he was simply a wounded man who had to be healed. That was our way of looking at it, and we treated him just the same way as the other patients. He gave us no trouble at all and was a very well behaved patient. He answered every question we put to him and gave us all the information we needed.

As to the stories about flowers and grapes being showered on him, they are just not true. There was no sentimentality about it at all; he was just a patient. If anyone spoilt him, and I am not saying they did, it was the soldiers. The boys treated him as a British soldier expects to treat a decent enemy.

I wondered at first what would be their reaction. I found they treated him normally, and when they had cigarettes he was invited to share them. At about this time we have an annual gift of cigarettes in memory of someone killed in India and the donor agreed that they should be distributed in the soldier's ward. Jerry had a packet the same as the others.

He is 22, married, and has a nine month old baby. His first thought when he came to hospital was to let his wife know that he was safe. When he was eventually able to send a prisoner of war letter he wrote that the food was excellent. When he first came to the hospital he was in a terrible state of fear. I have never seen such a look of terror in a man. He must have been drilled to believe in the most terrible things, which would happen to him, if he landed alive in England.

After two days of rest and quiet however he was quite different and realised he was being treated decently. He could not speak any English when he came but I was surprised at the amount he picked up while he was at the hospital. One of the Tommies bought him a 'Sally paper' in which there is a short column in German".

If this patient were Helmut Glaser, then he would obviously have been the last one sent to the Canadian Prisoner of War camp. The three airmen remained in captivity until 1946 and then I would imagine they returned to Germany. The two airmen who were killed, Albert Weber and Johannes Moorfeld, were presumably kept at Worthing Hospital until they were buried at Durrington Cemetery five days later on Wednesday 21st August 1940.

The Worthing Herald, dated Friday 23rd August stated that; Two German airmen, Johannes Moorfeld and Albert Weber, who were killed in a recent air battle over the south east coast, were given a military funeral on Wednesday. The two simply made oak coffins were carried to the graves by men of the famous infantry regiment, the chaplain of which conducted the funeral service. Before the coffins were placed in the graves, the German flag, with a huge black swastika in the middle, was draped over them, and the chaplain read the last rites. As the coffins were being carried to the graves a number of British fighters flew over the cemetery. A three round salute was given to the dead men by the firing party, which was under a regimental sergeant major.

The photograph, which appeared with the article, can be seen above.
(Worthing Herald and Gazette / Portsmouth Publishing and Printing Ltd)

Unteroffizier Albert Weber (58246/123) can be seen below. He was born in
Papenhofen, Germany on 18-09-10 and was the oldest member of
the G1+FR Heinkel crew. (Mr S. Hall / Johannes Weber)

On Wednesday 28th August the Worthing Gazette also covered the burial of Johannes Moorfeld and Albert Weber. It was explained in the same way as the Worthing Herald but they also added that the Nazi airmen were the first enemy casualties to be buried in the soldiers, sailors and airmen's corner of the cemetery.

It appears as though the burial of Germans in local cemeteries at the time was quite controversial. A letter published in the Worthing Herald, titled "Burial of German Airmen" on Friday 30th August 1940 regarding the burial of Johannes Moorfeld and Albert Weber is a great example.

The Herald reader stated that; "The picture and statement in your last issue of a British army chaplain conducting a religious memorial service of two German airmen with the anti-Christ Swastika flag given a place of honour and prominence is both horrifying and astounding; also that our army with its high principled motives should be identified with the firing of a salute in honour at the same ceremony of such barbarous pagans is petrifying.

How can God's holy name be evoked in death if it has been blasphemed in life? Hitler has said that one is either a German or a Christian, you can not be both. A German Minister of church affairs stated three years ago; "The primacy of the state over the church must be recognised. A new authority, Adolf Hitler, has arisen as to what Christ and Christianity really are. The German faith movement embodies the following sentiments. It fights for an exclusively German education without any Christian adjuncts".

The Herald reader continues; Our Lord God Almighty is Holy and all that do unrighteously are an abomination unto the Lord thy God (Deuteronomy 25-10). He that justifieth the wicked and he that condemneth the just, even they both are abomination to the Lord (Proverbs 17-10). Even the prayers of those who reject Gods laws are abomination to him (Proverbs 28-9).

One is astonished that any professing Christian could presume to conduct a Christian religious service over the German pagan flag or countenance such procedure".

Also in the same Worthing Herald as the above, dated Friday 30th August 1940 was another interesting letter titled "Are we Christian". The Herald reader explained; "None the less it seems a pity that in some of us the Christian virtues seem to go by the board in moments of stress.

There were incidents connected with the crashing of an enemy aeroplane some little time ago which made one wonder whether, after all, this country is as Christian as we would like to believe. An overwhelming desire to see the fallen enemy at close quarters is understandable but individuals, some of them professing Christians, should gloat over the blood stained uniform of a dead fellow creature, killed doing what he conceived to be his duty, is almost unbelievable.

But it happened, and some of the remarks made about the crew of that particular aeroplane were equally unchristian. It is undoubtedly, very difficult to love your enemies, but it hardly becomes Christian to abuse them when they are dead or incapacitated. The Swastika is a pagan symbol, and they're all pagans, said a respectable fellow citizen the other day. I think he would almost have gone to the length of denying our enemies a Christian burial.

It is interesting to note that our enemies are not all pagans. One of them, at any rate, now lying wounded in hospital, is a member of the Evangelical Church of Germany. He has left a wife and baby son behind him, and is, by the way, very popular with the other patients in the ward. That he was and is an enemy of the country and of most of the things we hold dear is undeniable that fellow Christians should damn him out of hand as a pagan because he has been caught up in the wheels of a war machine is surely in direct opposition to the injunctions of our Lord".

I was very pleased that the Worthing Herald and Gazette gave me permission to use these letters. What is interesting is the way these letters have been worded. Some of the words shown are very strong and it just goes to show how deeply some people felt about this incident.

Early one morning, during the mid-1960's Johannes Moorfeld and Albert Weber were exhumed from Section 2, Row 16, Graves 23 and 26. Fifteen other German airmen who were also killed during the Second World War in crashes local to Worthing were also quietly exhumed from Durrington Cemetery and were all taken approximately 215 miles north to the Cannock Chase German Military Cemetery in Cannock, Staffordshire.

The aim was to enable the German Authorities to ensure that the graves, scattered in cemeteries all over England, would be properly looked after. Johannes Moorfeld now lies in Block 4 Grave 220 and Albert Weber now lies in Block 4 Grave 240.

The names of the 17 German airmen exhumed from Durrington Cemetery can be seen below. These men were all buried between 1940 and 1943.

A. Weber, J. Moorfeld, G. Buscher, G. Reinsburg, F. Puschel, H. Jansen, J. Richter, A. Kielmann, F. Dolezal, R. Ertel, H. Prang, E. Schnuppel, E. Sassenroth, G. Grussner, H. Grosse-Heitmeyer, J. Kratsch, V. Piering.

Although it was the German Authorities intention to exhume all German servicemen who were killed and buried in cemeteries across England, the funding for this major task eventually ran dry and so many still remain in their original resting place.

Littlehampton Cemetery and Tangmere Cemetery near Chichester are no exception. Both cemeteries still have well maintained sections for German airmen killed during the war and are situated just feet from the final resting places of British and Commonwealth war dead.

A photograph of the German graves at Tangmere Cemetery.
(Authors Collection)

Durrington Cemetery as it is today. (Authors Collection)

The photograph below shows the soldiers, sailors and airman's corner where Johannes Moorfeld and Albert Weber were originally buried on Wednesday 21st August 1940. (Authors Collection)

I decided to pay a visit to the Cannock Chase German Military Cemetery. This was the large stone tablet, which greeted me before I went in to locate the graves of Albert Weber and Johannes Moorfeld. (Authors Collection)

A photograph showing the general layout of the cemetery can be seen below.
(Authors Collection)

In the cemetery rest 2143 soldiers from the First World War along with another 90 who are unknown. From the Second World War lie 2786 and another 5 who are unknown. All died on British territory.

Since visiting the site I have been told that the five unknown bodies buried at Cannock Chase could have been girlfriends of crewmen. Although very uncommon, I am told that some crewmen asked their girlfriends if they wished to join them for a trip to England. I would imagine however, that once it was established that many planes were not returning, that this idea stopped immediately.

This photograph shows the grave of Albert Weber. All gravestones share two names, however the bodies are laid in two separate graves alongside of each other. I was very surprised at first when I learnt that Albert Weber and Johannes Moorfeld were not buried next to each other. I thought that men who died in the same incident would probably be kept together. It does seem however as though this is not the case. (Authors Collection)

A photograph showing the grave of Johannes Moorfeld. Incidentally, Georg Buscher and Gerhard Reinsburg, whose names share the gravestones with Albert Weber and Johannes Moorfeld, were also originally buried at Durrington Cemetery. They were both killed, along with F. Puschel in the L1+MB Junkers 88 crash at Greyfriars Lane in Storrington, West Sussex on 2nd November 1940. For more information on this crash see "The Chanctonbury Crashes" by Martin F. Mace, published by The Historic Military Press. (Authors Collection)

Crash Site Map

Not only does this map show the crash site, it also shows Durrington Cemetery where Johannes Moorfeld and Albert Weber were first buried.

Due to the witnesses on Friday 16th August 1940 I have been able to approximately mark the Heinkel's course before it crash-landed. This can be seen if one follows the line of dots coming from West Worthing, passing over Offington Corner, heading north and disappearing off the map for approximately one mile. As explained previously the Heinkel's course then turned southwest. From here it appears back on the map, passes over Rogers farm, then Honeysuckle Lane and crash lands in the field near Cote Street.

Sadly due to copyright issues I was forced to sketch this map myself, however I believe it to be fairly accurate and to scale.

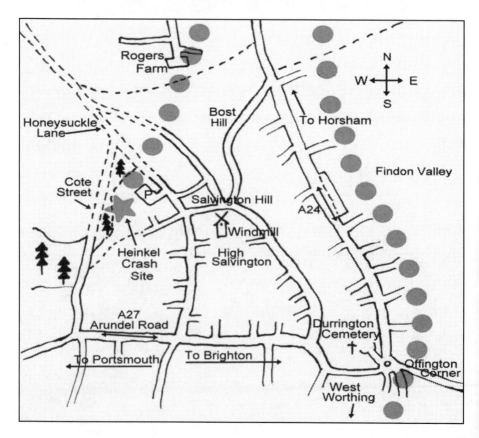

Kampfgeschwader 55

Kampfgeschwader 55 "Greif" (KG55) (Battle Wing 55) was one of the Luftwaffe's most famous bomber units. It was also the unit, which brought the High Salvington Heinkel over to England.

The Kampfgeschwader 55 "Greif" emblem.
(Foerderverein des Luftwaffenmuseums der Bundeswehr)

The history of KG55 dates back to April 1934 and was one of the first Luftwaffe units to be given Ernst Heinkel's advanced bomber, the He111. Initially based at Fassberg, many aircrew were first involved with the "Condor Legion" during the Spanish Civil War.

In September 1939, KG55 was involved in the attack on Poland, although the unit withdrew once Poland's capital, Warsaw, capitulated on 27th September 1939. KG55 was moved back to airfields in Germany in preparation for the attack on France, which began in October 1939 and went on until 25th June 1940, when France also capitulated. The bomber unit then became involved in the Battle of Britain and later, the Blitz.

Having achieved low cost victories in the first ten months of the war, the airmen of KG55 were extremely confident, although this would soon change. At the start of the Battle of Britain initial losses were light, losing seven aircraft in July 1940, however losses were to mount and the Geschwader would lose some of its most experienced crews. Between 10th July and 31st October 1940, KG55 lost 73 planes due to enemy action.

In July 1941 many units of KG55 withdrew and began operations on the Russian Front, where they would be involved for the next four years. They would start by providing air support for Army Group South attacking into the Ukraine in its drive towards the Caucasus and the Soviet oil fields. The Luftwaffe established air superiority after destroying and capturing over 4,000 Soviet aircraft in the first weeks of the invasion.

During the stalemate of the winter 1941/42 the units of KG55 were redeployed to rest in western France and did not return until April 1942. KG55 was again deployed to the Ukraine, although on this occasion would support the 11th Army in the Crimea and the 6th Army pushing its way eastward from the Charkow area into the Caucasus.

KG55 supported German forces throughout 1943 and was heavily involved in Operation Citadel. By 10th May 1944, KG55 had completed its 50,000[th] mission. In 1945 all units of KG55 were withdrawn from front line duty and the unit was then disbanded.

Amazingly enough the Heinkel bomber was kept by KG55 as its principal machine for the entire war and even in the dying days of Hitler's Reich, the latest variants of the He111 were still in active service on the Russian Front. Incidentally production of the Heinkel ceased in 1944.

For more information on Kampfgeschwader 55, see "KG55" by Steve Hall and Lionel Quinlan, published by Red Kite.

The Spitfire Pilot and 602 Squadron

Although other members of 602 Squadron were initially involved in the High Salvington Heinkel chase, it was Robert Findlay Boyd who was credited with the "kill". He was born in East Kilbride, Scotland on 8th June 1916. He worked as a Mining Engineer prior to the war and joined 602 Squadron (City of Glasgow) Auxiliary Air Force in 1935. He was not mobilised with the squadron however until the end of 1939.

The 602 Squadron crest. Cave Leonem Cruciatum –
Beware the Tormented Lion. (The 602 Squadron Museum Association)

The Squadron was formed on 12th September 1925 at Moorpark Aerodrome at Renfrew in Scotland as a day bomber unit. Initially equipped with DH9A's, they were replaced with Fawns in September 1927, which in turn were replaced by the Wapitis in 1929.

Harts were then used from February 1934 and the squadron re-equipped with Hinds in June 1936. On the 1st November 1938 the squadron was changed to an army co-operation squadron, but on the 14th January 1939 this was changed once again to become a fighter unit. During this time the aircraft were changed to Gauntlets.

602 were the first auxiliary squadron to be given Spitfires, which were delivered on 8th May 1939 and as a result became the seventh squadron in the whole of the Royal Air Force to have them. On 24th August 1939 they were embodied into the RAF in anticipation of the outbreak of war. They were commanded by Squadron Leader Douglas Farquhar at RAF Abbotsinch (now Glasgow Airport), with a total strength of 22 Officers and 174 airmen.

602 Squadron were involved in the shooting down of the very first German bomber, a Junkers 88, on Monday 16th October 1939, which crashed in the Firth of Forth. The pilot was captured and although pulled from the sea unconscious, he died shortly afterwards. It has been a long source of argument as to whether it was 602 or 603 (City of Edinburgh) Squadron who actually got this first "kill" of the war, but reports strongly support 602's claim.

On Saturday 28th October 1939 they were also involved in shooting down the first German aircraft to crash on the British Isles (rather than into the sea) during the Second World War. This was a Heinkel 111 and landed at Long Newton's Farm, Humbie, near Edinburgh. Two crewmen were killed in the incident, although two others were captured.

In August 1940 the squadron moved southwards from Scotland to the newly opened RAF airfield at Westhampnett in West Sussex and by this time Robert Findlay Boyd had become a Flight Lieutenant. Westhampnett airfield had a grass runway and being located approximately 1.5 miles NNE of Chichester it became part of the Tangmere sector.

Soon after settling in, 602 Squadron was to be involved in the Battle of Britain and Boyd was to shoot down a large number of enemy aircraft. His first "kill" in Sussex was a Dornier 215 on Thursday 15th August 1940.

The photograph shown below was taken outside the Officers mess at RAF Westhampnett in November 1940. Boyd can be seen seated in the front row, second in from the left, with the dog lying in front of him.
(Mr D. Rowland)

Due to the skill of the pilots, 602 squadron established a leading reputation, finishing the conflict with the second highest total of "kills". They also boasted the lowest total of "pilot loss rate" as well as being the longest serving squadron in the front line.

The photograph shown above, taken from under the wing of a Spitfire, was taken shortly after arriving at Westhampnett. It shows the airfield ready for the call to action. (Mr D. Rowland)

The photograph below was also taken at Westhampnett during the height of the Battle of Britain in 1940. (Mr D. Rowland)

On 2nd October 1940 Boyd shared a Junkers 88 with his colleague, Patrick Barthropp of 602 Squadron. Intercepted as it approached the coast of Shoreham, West Sussex, it was chased out to sea and shot down 35 miles out. Incidentally, Patrick, known as "Paddy", was shot down in 1942 over France and became a prisoner of war. He was assigned to Stalag Luft III, the camp made famous by the film "The Great Escape", starring Steve McQueen, James Garner and Richard Attenborough. He was in one of the huts ready to take his turn, but after 76 men had escaped from the camp the German guards finally found out what they were up to. He was released and sent back to England in May 1945.

Robert Findlay Boyd's final victory in 1940 was a shared Junkers 88 on 13th November. He was awarded the "DFC" (Distinguished Flying Cross) on the 24th September 1940 for nine victories, and a Bar on the 25th October 1940 for a further three victories.

The official war artist, Cuthbert Orde drew his picture that same month at Westhampnett. The drawings were free to senior pilots, but any lower ranking pilots, pilot officers and sergeants had to pay for their picture out of their own wages. The cost was five pounds, but because Robert Findlay Boyd was a senior pilot, he was fortunate to have his for free. As each pilot sat down to be drawn he had to brace himself for some pointed remarks from his colleagues. When it was Boyd's turn, his friends said "See if he can draw in some hair for you Findlay" – for Boyd was fast losing his.

The portrait of Flight Lieutenant Robert Findlay Boyd can be seen below.
(Crown Copyright / Ministry of Defence)

In December 1940 Boyd was given command of 54 Squadron at Catterick, a position he held until July 1941. Later that year he was posted to 58 OTU at Grangemouth, and then to 57 OTU where he was promoted wing commander. In February 1942 he was on a patrol with his group captain Victor Beamish when they spotted the famous German Capital ships "Scharnhorst" and the "Gneisenau" steaming along the English Channel. They quickly returned to England to raise the alarm.

The citation for Boyd's "DSO" (Distinguished Service Order) in April 1942 stated that he had destroyed a total of twenty-one enemy aircraft. He had also shared the loss of seven aircraft, had three probables and had damaged seven. In 1943 he commanded Eglington airfield for a period. Later that year he was sent out to the Far East AHQ, Bengal and from there he was posted to command 293 Wing on the Burma front at the beginning of April 1944. He made many claims to have shot down Japanese aircraft while there, but no confirmation has been found of this.

He retired from the RAF in 1945, as a Group Captain. Boyd flew charter flights for Scottish Aviation, later tried pig farming and herring fishing and then moved to the Isle of Skye, where he kept the Ferry Inn at Uig. He sadly died in April 1975.

602 Squadron was disbanded on 15th May 1945, by which time they were credited with the destruction of 150 enemy aircraft. After the war had finished 602 Squadron was reformed in its auxiliary state, flying Spitfires from Abbotsinch and, for a time, Renfrew. In January 1951 the Spitfires gave way to Vampire jet aircraft which were flown until final disbandment of the squadron in January 1957.

602 Squadron however has not been forgotten. On 21st May 1982 an association was formed and a museum created at the Headquarters of 2175 (Rolls Royce) Squadron Air Training Corps at Hillington, Glasgow. Today, the museum has moved from this site and can be found in Glasgow City centre. Robert Findlay Boyd's son, John Boyd, is a member of the 602 Squadron Association and as a result I was able to speak to him about my research. He was kind enough to send me some useful material for me to use from his home on the Isle of Skye.

For more information on 602 Squadron see "Spitfires over Sussex" by David Rowland, published by Finsbury Publishing.

A photograph of Westhampnett airfield as it is today. (Authors Collection)

Now known as Goodwood it is used purely for pleasure flights. The Goodwood motor racing circuit surrounds the airfield. (Authors Collection)

Documents

The following pages show documentation, which support the High Salvington Heinkel incident. Robert Findlay Boyd's RAF Combat Report can be seen below. (The National Archives)

SECRET.   FORM F

COMBAT REPORT.

Sector Serial No. (A)	
Serial No. of Order detailing Flight or Squadron to Patrol (B)	
Date (C)	16 . 8 . 40 .
Flight, Squadron (D)	Flight : Blue Sqdn. : 602 .
Number of Enemy Aircraft (E)	One .
Type of Enemy Aircraft (F)	HE 111
Time Attack was delivered (G)	1655 hrs .
Place Attack was delivered (H)	5 miles N of Worthing .
Height of Enemy (J)	2,500'
Enemy Casualties (K)	One . HE 111 destroyed
Our Casualties Aircraft (L)	Nil .
Personnel (M)	Nil .
GENERAL REPORT N.1 N/A N.2 N/A (R)	

(R) P. Above Aslew & Above Beam 9 000 yards from
the aircraft of Section.

p. Sighted E.A. approx. 1000 ft above and coming towards us. Blue 1 did climbing turn and delivered beam attack. Followed by Blue II who stopped one motor. Successive attacks were delivered by Section until E.A. crashed in waste ground approx Heinkel North of Worthing.
landed 1745h.

Signature R. Boyd. Flt.

O.C. B Section
              Flight
              Squadron   Squadron No. 602 .

- 50 -

The RAF Intelligence Report concerning the High Salvington Heinkel can be seen below and is purposely shown on its side to make full use of the page. Note the incorrect registration of the plane, G1+SR. All other reports for the High Salvington Heinkel show the correct registration G1+FR. (Mr C. Ellis)

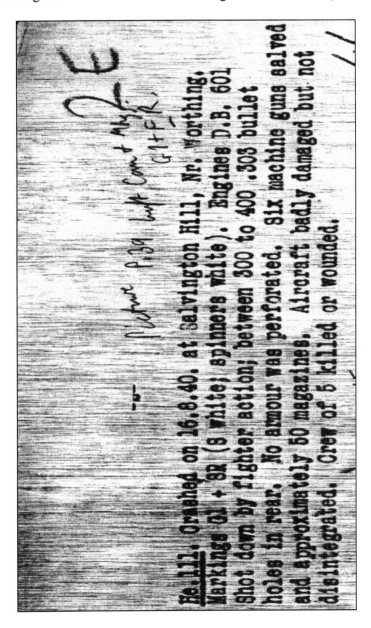

The Luftwaffe filled out a Loss Return Document if personnel failed to return. The crew of Heinkel G1+FR can be seen in the document below. (Mr S. Hall)

III./K.G. 55

lfd. Nr.	Ort und Tag des Gefechts	Staffel usw.	Dienstgrad	Vorname	Familienname, Truppenteil, Fz. des Erkennungsmarke		Geburts-g	
						Tag	Monat	Kreis
1	2	3	4	5	6	7	8	9
1	Bei ... auf Reading am 16... bei Fri...	Leutnant Flg.- Fhr.	Rudolf	Theopold III./K.G.55 58246/199	4 2 20			SCHÖNBERG
2	wie vor	wie vor	Uffz., Bo.Sch.	Rudolf	Horntostel III./K.G.55 58246/403	9 1 15		ETTENBÜTTEL
3	wie vor	wie vor	Gefr. Bofu.	Helmut	Glaser III./K.G.55 58246/126	9. 9. 18		Zörblitz
4	wie vor	wie vor	Uffz. Bome.	Albert	Weber III./K.G.55 58246/123	18. 9. 10		Papen- Höfen
5	wie vor	wie vor	Gefr. Bordsch.	Johannes	Moorfeld III./K.G.55 58246/411	3. 7. 17		Oester- wiehe

The opposite page of the document can be seen below.

10	Verwundet Körperfälle und Tod/Gefr		Vermißt		Gefecht außerhalb der Lazarett- behandlung infolge von				Abgeführt an welche Dienste des Jahres (Krankenhaus) und unabh.	Bemerkung (z.B. Beob- tage über bel. 17 — Deckb. I — vermutlich Umgekommen)
	schwer	leicht	gefangen	tod/flg	Unverw. wung	Krankh.	Selbst	Selbstmord		
10	11	12	13	14	15	16	17	18	19	20
			vermißt seit 16.8.40		*in Canada*				*briefw. Anzeige Gef. 4.9.*	Bei Angriff auf Flugplatz Heathrow
			wie vor						*briefw. Gef. LH 10.9 in Canada*	wie vor
			wie vor						*briefw. Gef. LP 30.8 in Canada*	wie vor
	gefallen		wie vor						*afo LP 12.12*	wie vor
	gefallen		wie vor						*afo LP 20.1.41*	wie vor

The Burial in War Grave's document containing the details of the first
burial of Johannes Moorfeld and Albert Weber can be seen below.
(Worthing Crematorium and Cemeteries)

The opposite page of the document can be seen below.

Souvenirs

It is fantastic to know that so many souvenirs taken from the High Salvington Heinkel still survive today and as a result I have been fortunate to be able to photograph many of these and to hear the owners accounts of that Friday afternoon in August 1940.

As explained in the introduction, my grandfather was also fortunate to visit the crash site and like many others, came home with souvenirs which had been taken from the German bomber. However his account on the High Salvington Heinkel goes right back to the beginning, as follows; "In the early evening of Friday 16th August 1940 my friend and I, both 16 years of age at the time, were watching a dog fight from Offington Lane, Worthing.

We had heard the air raid sirens go off minutes before, but there were no shelters in the vicinity to take cover. Suddenly a German Heinkel bomber flew over, heading north towards the village of Findon and was being riddled with machine gun fire by a RAF Spitfire in hot pursuit".

This photograph shows Offington Lane, as it is today, heading north with Offington Avenue on the right. The Land Rover Discovery on the right obscures the corner where my grandfather and his friend stood as the planes flew over. (Authors Collection)

My grandfather continued; "We both leapt onto our bikes and peddled like crazy to keep up with the action. By the time we got to Offington Corner we could see in the far distance the two planes turning in a south-westerly direction and heading towards High Salvington.

Dramatically losing height we both watched as the Heinkel, evidently preparing to ditch, disappeared over the back of High Salvington closely followed by the RAF Spitfire. We rode up Crockhurst Hill and carried on westwards along the Arundel road, now better known as the A27 and then turned right up Salvington Hill.

It was completely by chance that we discovered the Heinkel, which had come down in a field between Honeysuckle Lane and Cote Street. When we arrived, the Home Guard and several policemen were already at the scene. There was a lot of talk and speculation about various issues within the large crowd and so at the time we didn't know what to believe. We had got there just in time to see two of the German airmen taken away, although the others had apparently been taken away seconds before.

My friend and I could not resist taking something from the plane as a souvenir and so I pulled some armoured cable from the cockpit and also ripped off two pieces of the aluminium fuselage. My friend however went home with the leather off one of the seats. When I returned home I scratched all the details on the back of the metal in order not to forget the incident. I did wonder what my friend would use the leather for, but all became apparent when he turned up one day with a strong, nicely made leather bag which had been hand stitched together by himself. The leather was good quality and very tough indeed".

During 2005 my grandfather found his Heinkel souvenirs and called me straight away. Not having seen them for many years I had forgotten that there were two pieces of fuselage and a length of armoured cable. We placed the souvenirs on the kitchen table and studied them carefully. Once we were finished with them they were returned to the old biscuit tin in which they were stored.

My grandfather has not seen his old friend for many years and believes that he is no longer with us, but explained that at one time the unique hand stitched leather bag was kept in his friend's garden shed. It is unknown if the leather bag exists today but I just hope the bag has remained in the family and that the story that goes with it has been passed on.

My grandfather, Eric Kennard, can be seen below holding his souvenirs at the Heinkel crash site in March 2005. This was the first time my grandfather had visited the site since the incident on Friday 16th August 1940.
(Authors Collection)

The armoured cable, which was taken from the cockpit, can also be seen.
(Authors Collection)

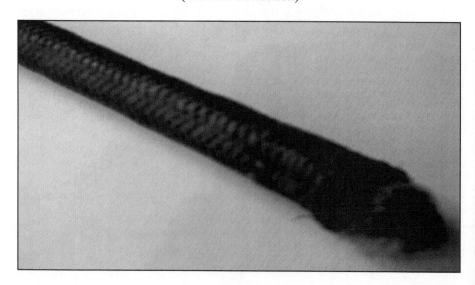

The two pieces of aluminium fuselage can be seen below. (Authors Collection)

The two pieces of aluminium are shown again but in this instance, showing the opposite side with the details my grandfather scratched into the surface. (Authors Collection)

Mrs B. Knight of Worthing remembers the incident but explains that being a girl, she was not allowed up to the crash site. However, shortly after, she obtained a clear perspex ring with three blue stones from a member of the Home Guard who had to stand guard over the plane. Mrs Knight explained that several of these rings were made but was not sure which part of the plane had been used to make them.

My only suggestion was that it was probably made from a sheet of perspex glazing. The Heinkel had a lot of this, most noticeably at the front of the plane. Clear perspex was used for two reasons. One, it was lighter than glass and two, if a bullet was to pass through it, or if the plane was to crash, the perspex would either crack or splinter and not smash into thousands of pieces.

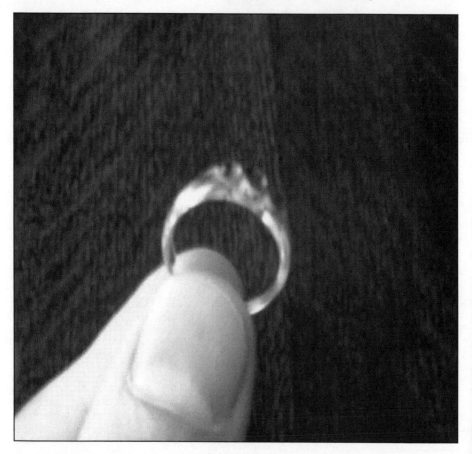

Mrs Knight's souvenir can be seen above. (Authors Collection)

The souvenir seen below was also taken from the plane by a member of the Home Guard. Worthing resident Geoffrey B. Winton explained to me that his grandfather, Arthur Pope had fought at Dunkirk but shortly after returning to England joined the Home Guard. While guarding the High Salvington Heinkel he was able to obtain this piece of fuselage. (Authors Collection)

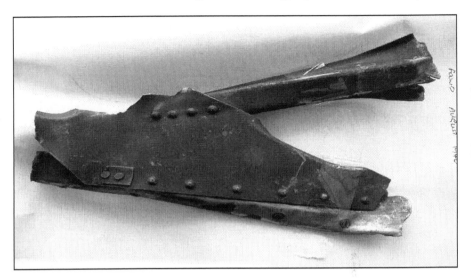

Interestingly enough while walking over the crash site nearly one year later, he was able to find another piece of the German bomber. This can be seen below. (Authors Collection)

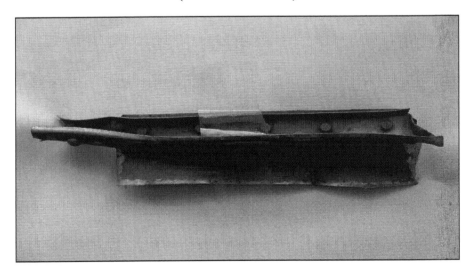

This interesting souvenir was taken by High Salvington resident,
William Wyatt. (Authors Collection)

Talking to Clive Lewis in Ferring, he explained that his grandfather, William,
lived in Honeysuckle Lane at the top of High Salvington. The Heinkel crash
site was right on his doorstep and as a result he was one of the first there.

It is not clear how Mr Wyatt knew that the Heinkel had come down, although it
is likely he heard the Spitfire's machine guns firing and then an almighty thud
as the German bomber hit the ground. The noise of the plane, cutting its way
through 400 yards of grass, mud and prickly gorse before coming to rest at the
hedgerow at the bottom of the field near Cote Street was also a sound many
would never forget or hear again.

When Mr Wyatt arrived he watched as the story unfolded. He wanted a
souvenir to take home but felt that there was too much going on and knowing
that the Army, Home Guard and Police were on the scene was not sure if he
would get away with taking something from the plane. He decided to go home
empty handed but with the intention of returning later.

Mr Lewis explained to me that his grandfather did exactly that and returned
later that day, and also seems to remember that his grandfather found no one
there, not even the Home Guard.

Records do show that a member of the Home Guard was placed at the Heinkel crash site 24 hours a day, obviously being relieved by another guard at intervals until the plane was taken away. I can only presume that at the time when Mr Wyatt arrived, there was a short gap in between shifts when no one stood guard.

A closer view of Mr Wyatt's souvenir. The word Sauerstoff, which can be seen on the neck of the cylinder simply means oxygen in English.
(Authors Collection)

Once Mr Wyatt had established that no one was around he climbed inside the plane, found a souvenir and then returned home. His find was a large aluminium oxygen cylinder, which had a screw cap and two valves at the top. He later found a good use for the souvenir and once he had sealed the valves at the top, the cylinder then became a hot water bottle which the family used for many years.

This photograph shows the other side of the aluminium cylinder, which is slightly larger than a 2-litre fizzy drink bottle. (Authors Collection)

Mr E. Richardson, who now lives in Walton on Thames, Surrey, also remembers the incident and still has his piece of the German bomber. Mr Richardson kindly sent me a letter which explained that his family lived at 36 North Street, Worthing from 1894 until the road widening scheme in the mid 1980's.

Mr Richardson recalls that the bus company, Southdown Motor Services ran special excursions to see the High Salvington Heinkel. His mother took him to the site and Mr Richardson being only 5½ years of age, found it all very exciting. When the Home Guard were otherwise distracted, he picked up a piece of the Heinkel, which he believed to be a piece of wing. When he returned home his father wrote on the back in capital letters "Piece of wing, Heinkel bomber 111 shot down 16/8/40".

Mr Richardson very kindly sent me his souvenir for photographing. One of the photographs can be seen below which shows the top surface. Note the spring-loaded Slot/fastener catch on the left. (Authors Collection)

Mr Richardson also vividly recalls seeing the sky filled with condensation trails and aircraft on a number of occasions during the summer of 1940 when the Battle of Britain was at its height. A year later he started St George's Church of England School.

This school was very close to the Gas works, which was an ideal target for enemy aircraft. Many families therefore decided to remove their children and place them into other schools in the area. Mr Richardson was sent to Christ Church and then later onto Sussex Road.

Another photograph of Mr Richardson's Heinkel souvenir can be seen above. This photograph is of the other side. One can see the details, which were written by his father, A.S. Richardson. The spring-loaded slot/fastener catch can be seen on the right. (Authors Collection)

Gary Harding of St Michael's Road, Worthing allowed me to photograph his High Salvington Heinkel souvenir. Mr Harding acquired it from a friend's grandfather, who, knowing he was interested in the subject, gave the switch to him. Mr Harding believes the switch may have been used for switching on and off the Heinkel's landing lights. (Authors Collection)

The opposite side of the switch can be seen below. (Authors Collection)

I was interested to learn that a local collector, Charles Edward George Clout, also had one of these switches from the Heinkel and was invited round to his Worthing home to view and photograph the switch. The switch can be seen below and although it appears to be identical to the switch in Gary Harding's collection, there are some differences. (Authors Collection)

The most noticeable differences are the staggered cubed contacts seen here on the left of the switch. (Authors Collection)

I may have been surprised to see another switch, but Mr Clout had another High Salvington souvenir to show me. It turned out to be the actual work plate from the plane, showing many details such as plane type, make, works number (1582) and even where the Heinkel was built. (Authors Collection)

During my research I was also fortunate to visit the home of Worthing resident Keith Downer. I was fascinated with his wartime stories, which have been well documented in many folders. It soon became apparent that Mr Downer was a keen historian and having cycled up to see the High Salvington Heinkel as a young lad, was able to retrieve a documented account of what he had seen that day.

Mr Downer passed me his account which explained that; "Several friends and I took our bikes up to High Salvington in order to see the aircraft. There she lay this big aircraft, silent, with that very strange smell of dope and fuel. The big green aircraft just lay there surrounded by an armed guard and hundreds of spectators. People were tearing pieces of metal off the plane and I shall always remember the large glassed nose area giving such good visibility to the crew. I managed to obtain several pieces of the aircraft, rubber from the fuel tanks and pieces of green metal.

It was several days later and we were up there again watching the men cutting the aircraft up before taking it away to an aircraft dump near Horsham, then WHOOSH! She caught fire due to one of the workmen using a cutter. It did not take long before the Heinkel was covered in flames and dark brown oily smoke. By the time the fire brigade reached the scene the fire was all over and apart from the remains of the two engines there was very little left of the aircraft. And so the Heinkel was no more. She would drop no more bombs and for two of her crew, they would never see their homeland again.

Fifty-six years later I sat in my car just looking at that same spot. I then walked around the grass where she had laid so long ago. Now the grass had all grown up again, new bushes, no burnt area, no trace, just tranquillity as several ladies walked their dogs, children were playing where death had occurred. It was just a perfect English summer's day as it had been so long ago.

I got back in my car and just sat there again; my mind was working overtime. I looked up, a large German plane was coming in, her crew frightened and there she lay, her war over, crashed. I started my car and moved away. I could still hear the people and I could feel the excitement of 1940.

I looked up at the lovely blue sky as aircraft passed overhead from either Gatwick or Heathrow. No bombs for them, they were on holiday to Spain or Italy maybe. Who cares now? Who can even remember? But I remember that sunny Friday of August 16th 1940".

Keith Downer's souvenirs, can be seen below. These pieces show a combination of light and dark green paint and bare aluminium. (Authors Collection)

The remaining souvenir pieces are seen below. Note the two pieces of rubber taken from the fuel tanks. (Authors Collection)

Philip Long, once a Worthing resident, but now living in Hove also visited the crash site and explained that; "On a Friday afternoon in August 1940, a German Heinkel 111 came hedge hopping from the north down the course of Cote Street. The plane had been mauled by a RAF Spitfire.

A Royal Artillery gunner and assistant, who were manning the twin Lewis machine gun on the searchlight site, on the west side of Cote Street swiftly, came into action. The gunner's assistant was unable to keep clear of one of the gun barrels in time, as they swung round, he sustained an injury to one of his ear lobes as bullets went straight through one side of his tin helmet. The plane crash landed in bushes and was within sight of the Lewis gun emplacement. Three of the airmen were taken prisoner.

Two days later on the Sunday afternoon, about 150 sightseers surrounded the plane, which had been roped off. At about 4 o'clock the armed sentry on duty to guard the plane decided to leave without a replacement. This triggered the crowd to swarm on the plane and help themselves to souvenirs. Soon the swastika marking in the tail of the plane was being cut out with a hacksaw. Someone set off a release of what appeared to be compressed air and the crowd retreated in fear of an explosion, but soon returned having regained some courage. Within a few days a special unit dismantled the plane and transported the pieces away".

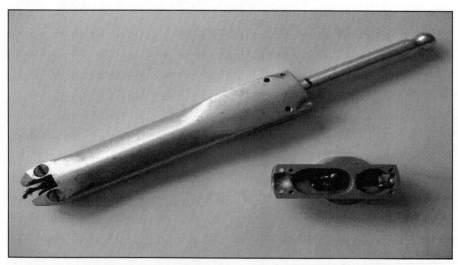

Mr Long's souvenirs, believed to be part of the bomb release can be seen above. (Authors Collection)

The High Salvington Heinkel's Kuvi bombsight could once be found on display at the Tangmere Military Aviation Museum near Chichester, West Sussex. The owner withdrew the souvenir from public display, where it was later sold on E-bay. Sadly its whereabouts today are not clear.

Two photographs of the bombsight are still held in the museum's archives and show both the front and the rear of the bombsight. The photograph showing the front can be seen below. (Tangmere Military Aviation Museum)

The photograph showing the opposite side of the bombsight can be seen below.
(Tangmere Military Aviation Museum)

These two photographs of 1940 Heinkel radio equipment were taken at the Amberley Working Museum near Arundel, West Sussex. (Authors Collection)

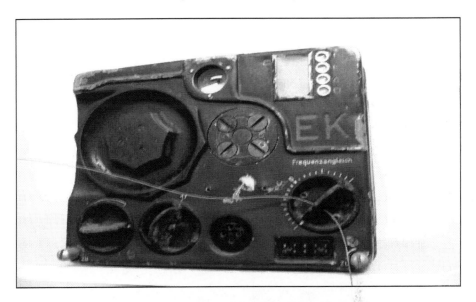

It is believed that one of these was taken from the High Salvington Heinkel, however this claim is not verified. (Authors Collection)

This photograph, found in the Historic Military Press archives, shows a piece of leather cut from one of the self-sealing fuel tanks. Several questions come to mind: Why has the leather been cut with such curves? What is the stitching all about? Is the stitching there just to give it a neat edge or is it to prevent the leather from tearing? So far I have been unable to answer these questions.
(Historic Military Press)

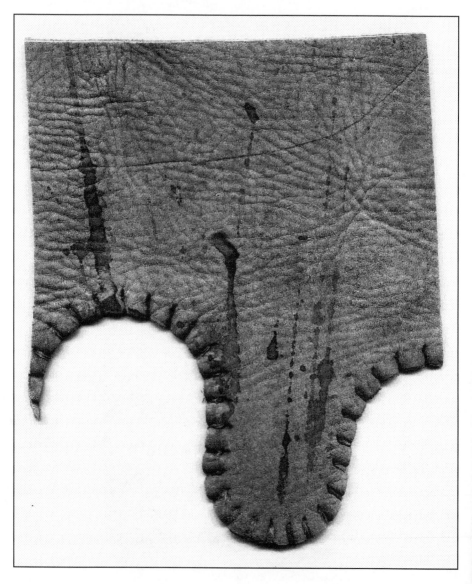

Co-author and Sussex aviation historian Pat Burgess also has a piece of leather cut from one of the self-sealing fuel tanks. A photograph of Pat can be seen below and shows him holding the souvenir piece in his garden in the early 1970's. The piece of leather is now half the length of that shown in the photograph due to many sections having been cut and exchanged for other Sussex aircraft crash parts. (Pat Burgess)

During a visit to Worthing Museum and Art Gallery, a member of staff informed me that they had a painting of the High Salvington Heinkel in their collection. I was able to make an appointment and returned to photograph the painting. Not much is known about the artist, who obviously found the crashed bomber an interesting subject.

It was painted in 1940 by N. O. Brown of Findon Valley, Worthing, using oil paint on a canvas mounted board and measures H 25.6 x W 36.0 cm. Strangely enough the Heinkel has been painted by the artist in battleship grey. These bombers were actually painted in a drab green and souvenir pieces of fuselage taken from the High Salvington Heinkel support this fact.

Perhaps the artist used the black and white photographs to paint from, which were published in the Worthing Herald and the Worthing Gazette a few days after the crash. As a result he would not have known the true colour of the plane. The painting was valued in 2003 at £400, though this was for insurance purposes only.

The painting by N. O. Brown. (Authors Collection)

The Crash Site Today

The crash site is easily accessible and is a favourite area for dog walkers. Parking in the car park at the top of Salvington Hill, one can find the area (owned by Worthing Borough Council) by walking southwest from the car park down the sloping field towards the hedgerow. A photograph of how the site looks today can be seen below. (Authors Collection)

The crash site on Friday 16th August 1940 - The Heinkel with the Home Guard present. Comparing the two photographs one can clearly see the two trees to the left of the picture and the field with the steady incline at the centre. (Worthing Herald and Gazette / Portsmouth Publishing and Printing Ltd)

Another view of the crash site as it is today can be seen below. One can clearly see how much the shrubbery has grown over the years. (Authors Collection)

Another view of the crash site on Friday 16th August 1940 - The photograph below shows a gap in the trees to the left of the tail. This can just about be found if one follows the tree line in the 2004 photograph.
(Worthing Herald and Gazette / Portsmouth Publishing and Printing Ltd)

Overview

Between the outbreak of war on 3rd September 1939 and 29th September 1944, air raid sirens wailed across Worthing 1,028 times due to enemy aircraft in the area. During these wartime years the Luftwaffe had dropped a total of 65 bombs on the town. I understand that 97 houses were destroyed and another 554 seriously damaged. A further 6,169 homes suffered minor damage. This does not include the thousands who had their windows blown out on more than one occasion. Many enemy planes were shot down in the area including one which crashed into a house in Lyndhurst Road.

Worthing and its people did not escape the evils of war and they played a vital role in support of the war effort. One has only got to look at the many books available about Worthing during wartime to be able to read the many stories and recollections from some of the townspeople. Despite all this and considering it happened all those years ago, the High Salvington Heinkel appears to be one of the most remembered incidents that occurred within the Borough of Worthing.

This particular German bomber may have come to an unfortunate end, however different variants of the Heinkel 111 can be found preserved throughout the world. One of these Heinkels sits quietly on display in the Battle of Britain hall at the RAF Museum at Hendon, London and I understand that this bomber is the only one in the Country. As for the Spitfire that shot the High Salvington Heinkel down, it finished active service and was later scrapped. Once again preserved variants can be found all over the world and prove to be very popular at air shows.

It has been suggested to Worthing Borough Council that a plaque should be placed at the crash site, explaining in brief, the incident. Other suggestions include a survey of the crash site to establish whether any Heinkel pieces may lie beneath the surface. These suggestions have been documented, however due to other financial priorities, it is unlikely that these will ever come to fruition.

My research on this downed German Heinkel 111P bomber has turned out to be far more in-depth than I ever imagined and although this book comes to an end I will continue to collect any information and/or unwanted souvenirs relating to this subject. As a result, I welcome any comments or additions.

Graham Lelliott

Further Reading

If you have been fascinated by this book you may also like to try;

"KG55, the Famous Luftwaffe Bomber Unit"
Written by Steve Hall and Lionel Quinlan. Published by Red Kite. 2000.

"The Chanctonbury Crashes"
Written by Martin F. Mace. Published by the Historic Military Press. 1998.

"German Fighters over the United Kingdom 1939-45"
Written by Alexander Nicoll. Published by the Historic Military Press. 2001.

"Battle over Sussex, 1940"
Written by Pat Burgess and Andy Saunders.
Published by Middleton Press. 1990.

"Blitz over Sussex, 1941-1942"
Written by Pat Burgess and Andy Saunders.
Published by Middleton Press. 1994.

"Bombers over Sussex, 1943-1945"
Written by Pat Burgess and Andy Saunders.
Published by Middleton Press. 1995.

"Battle of Britain"
Written by A. Price. Published by Arms and Armour Press. 1990.

"The Battle of Britain, Then and Now"
Written by W. Ramsey. Published by Plaistow Press. 1980.

"Spitfire Summer"
Written by P. Haining. Published by W.H. Allen and Co. 1990.

"Spitfires over Sussex"
Written by David Rowland. Published by Finsbury Publishing. 2000.

"Britain at War" Magazine
Published by Green Arbor Publishing on the 11th day of the proceeding month.

Acknowledgements

My sincere thanks go to the following people and sources used, especially those who have kindly given permission to use photographs and official documents;

Eric Kennard
Chris Sibley
Mike Franklin
Tim Yates
Geoff Gourd
Chris Willis
John Boyd
Johannes Weber
Peter Trounce
Freddie Feest
Clive Ellis
Gary Harding
Charles Edward George Clout
Brian Cracknell
Worthing Library
Worthing Hospital
Worthing Museum and Art Gallery
Worthing Crematorium and Cemeteries
Worthing Borough Council
The Worthing Herald and Gazette
The Worthing Argus and Sentinel
The West Sussex Gazette
Steve Hall, author of "KG55, the Famous Luftwaffe Bomber Unit"
David Rowland, author of "Spitfires over Sussex"
Martin Mace, author of "The Chanctonbury Crashes"
Andy Saunders and Pat Burgess, authors of "Battle over Sussex"
The Historic Military Press, Pulborough, West Sussex
Middleton Press, Midhurst, West Sussex
Portsmouth Publishing and Printing Ltd, West Sussex Division
The National Archives, Kew, Surrey
West Sussex Records Office, Chichester
The Hendon RAF Museum, Hendon, London
Amberley Working Museum, Amberley, West Sussex

The Imperial War Museum, London
The 602 Squadron Museum Association, Glasgow, Scotland
Tangmere Military Aviation Museum, Chichester, West Sussex
Goodwood Airfield and Motor Racing Circuit, Chichester, West Sussex
MOD Air Historical Branch, RAF Bentley Priory, Stanmore, Middlesex
Commonwealth War Graves Commission, Sydenham, Warwickshire
Cannock Chase German Military Cemetery, Cannock, Staffordshire
Crown Copyright / Ministry of Defence, London
The German Embassy, London
Roger Moulds, BBC WW2 People's War (Article A5947167)
Ronald Ham, BBC WW2 People's War (Article A1959311)
Foerderverein des Luftwaffenmuseums der Bundeswehr, Berlin, Germany
Volksbund Deutsche Kriegsgraberfursorge, Kassel, Germany
Bundesarchiv-Militararchiv, Freiburg im Breisgau, Germany

I would also like to thank the following local newspapers who kindly published
my High Salvington Heinkel inquiries in order to help me further this project
and to help me promote the first edition of this book;

Worthing Herald and Gazette.
Articles published in April 2004, August and September 2005, August 2006
and May 2007.

The Worthing Argus and Sentinel.
Articles published in November 2005, February and April 2006.

The West Sussex Gazette.
Articles published in December 2005 and April 2006.

As a result of these articles I would like to thank the following people who
replied with their own memories of the incident and to those who welcomed
me to photograph their High Salvington Heinkel souvenirs;

Bill Baldwin, Brian Chappell, Allen Woods, John Goodwin, Barbara Chipper,
Lionel Burns, Keith Downer, J. T. Harman, Albert Bassett, Bernard Wyatt,
Clive Lewis, B. Knight, G. Wheeler, Geoffrey B. Winton, Eric Richardson,
Alan Townsend, A. M. Hurst, Eric Reed, George Peace, Philip Long,
Ernie Parsons, John Sylvester, Evelyn Smith, Bob Richards and Valerie Kay.